In loving memory of Michelle Tooley and in support of everyone working for justice.

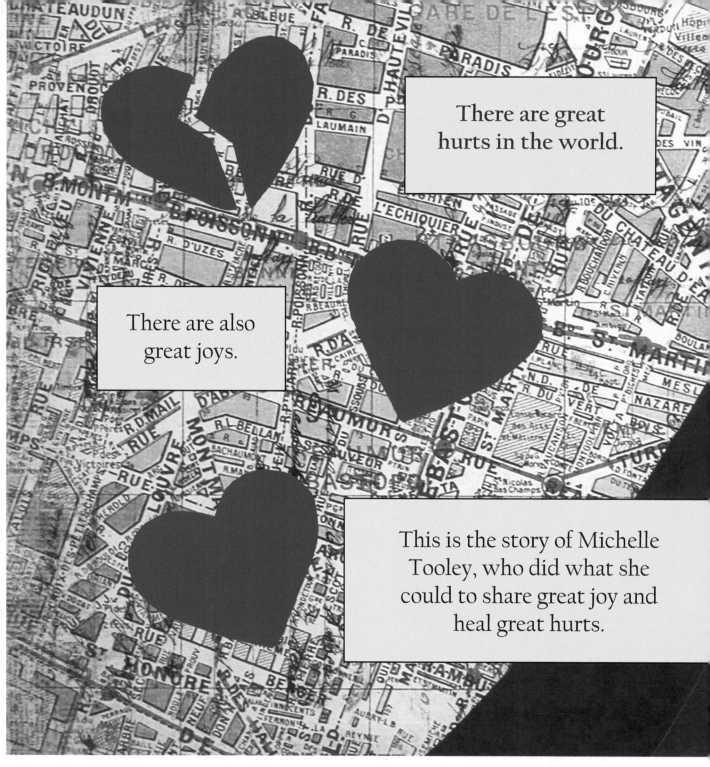

There are great hurts in the world.

There are also great joys.

This is the story of Michelle Tooley, who did what she could to share great joy and heal great hurts.

Michelle saw there were a lot of things that weren't right or kind or just.

She saw people who didn't have enough food or water.

She saw people mistreated based on how they looked.

She saw women underrepresented and silenced where important decisions were made.

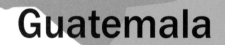

Guatemala

Nicaragua

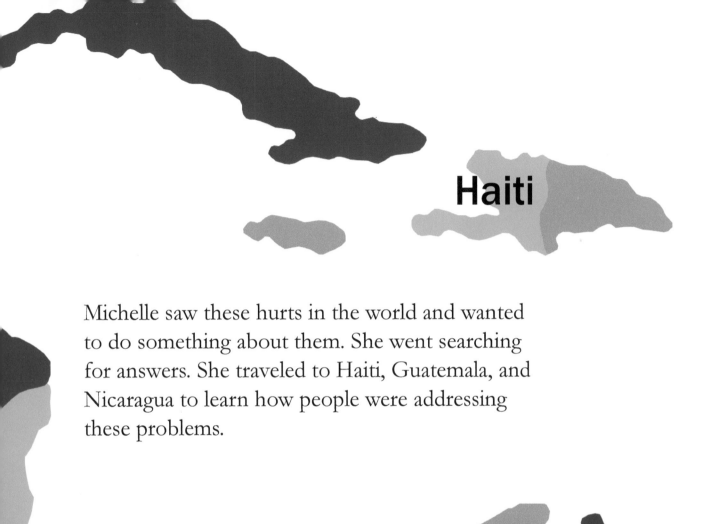

Haiti

Michelle saw these hurts in the world and wanted to do something about them. She went searching for answers. She traveled to Haiti, Guatemala, and Nicaragua to learn how people were addressing these problems.

As she traveled, she saw a lot of poverty and violence, but she also saw women coming together in groups, in churches, and in people's homes to find strength and hope in one another.

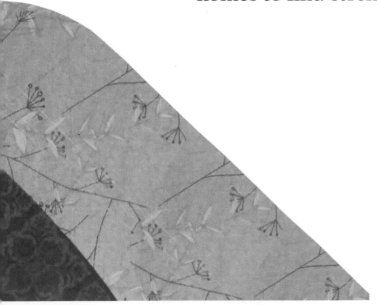

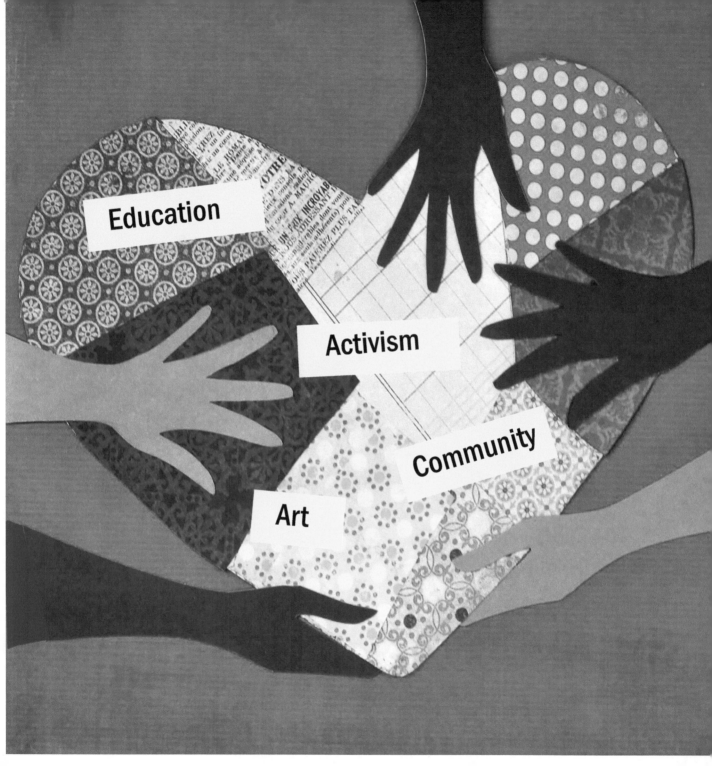

They worked together to make sure the voices and needs of the people were heard.

Michelle understood that these women had much to teach us about what it means to stand up for others when we know something isn't fair or just.

It's okay to ask for help.

In Haiti, while volunteering at an orphanage, Michelle thought about staying and continuing to work there.

The orphanage director and Michelle talked about her desire to stay.

He said, "You could work here, or you could go back to the U.S. and share our stories. Sharing them will help people see who we are and how we are working to help others."

Michelle took his advice to heart. She decided to return to the U.S. and share the stories of the people she met during her travels. She wanted to inspire people to take action to make their community and the world more fair and just.

In meetings with government officials, in living rooms, in classrooms, and on front porches, she challenged people to think about how to change the world.

Michelle wrote a book called *Voices of the Voiceless*. In it, she uplifted the experiences of women in Guatemala who had experienced war and pain, but kept working together and supporting each other, even when it felt impossible.

Inspired by the women she met in her travels, Michelle taught college students and pushed them to consider how they can help heal the hurts of the world.

She took students out of the classroom and down the street to work with the local food bank so they could learn about how laws could help or hurt people who were hungry.

She helped her students think about when and how to speak up and say, "Something is wrong here." She took them to protests where they gathered with other people from across the nation. She took them to other countries to meet leaders there and learn from them.

She provided a listening ear to her students, neighbors, and co-workers.

She celebrated their successes and supported them in times of need.

She recognized their strengths and brought them together to work on larger problems in the community.

Michelle noticed her college students had a gift for seeing the hurts in the world and finding creative ways to solve them. She wondered what would happen if she began nurturing those gifts in children.

She had the desire to start a camp where kids could learn skills to solve problems together, develop creative solutions, and make the world better, a little at a time.

Hurts in the world happen in so many ways. Sometimes people who do a lot of good get really sick. And one day Michelle became very sick.

But this did not stop her from spreading love and joy through stories.

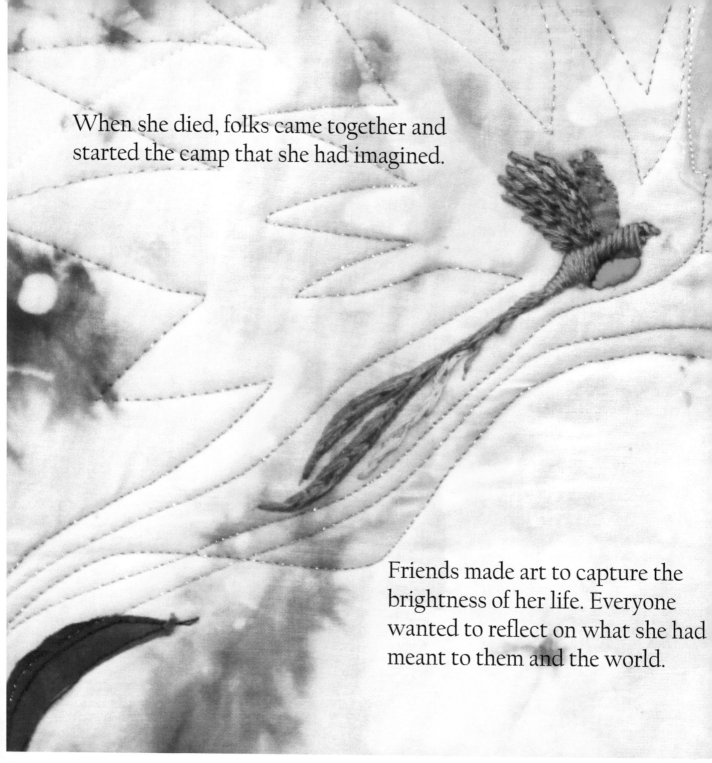

When she died, folks came together and started the camp that she had imagined.

Friends made art to capture the brightness of her life. Everyone wanted to reflect on what she had meant to them and the world.

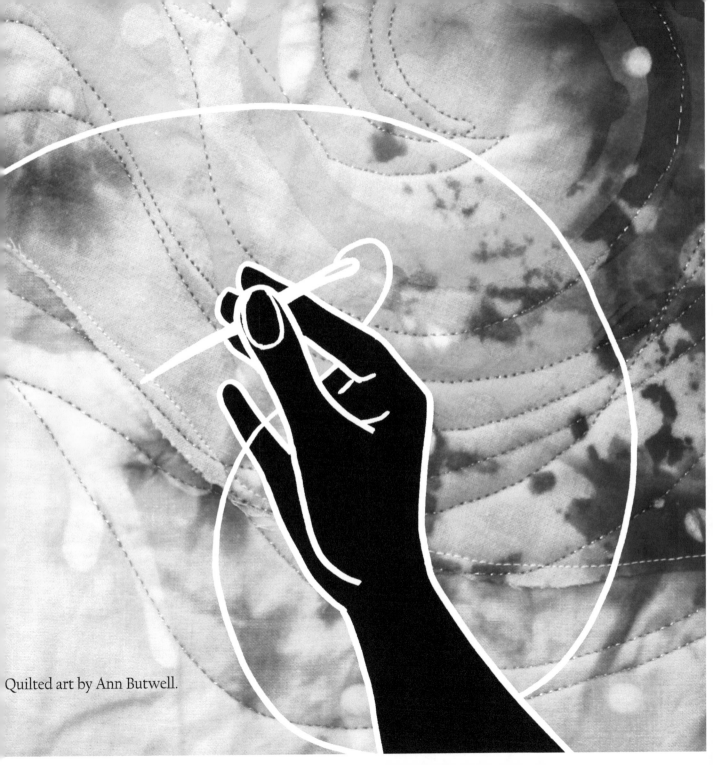

Quilted art by Ann Butwell.

When we work together, we are strong and creative enough to face even the biggest problems in this world.

Michelle inspired others to speak up when they saw problems, to work with others to make things right, and to always lend a listening ear.

We are
our best selves
when we
listen and learn
from others.

"Michelle is the one who taught me you can be a fighter and you can also be a peace builder."

- Meta Mendel-Reyes

Her class challenged my worldview but also made me feel like I belonged Berea.

- Rebecca Tucker

Halloween 2015

This evening, movie,
TV, and game figures walk
to and fro. Michelle,
your old home's carport glows.
Leaves blow and cars crawl along
the street: ninjas, cats,
And ghosts? Fewer. Maybe from
all the lives you loved.

Chris Green

ERFLIES

TED CHECKERSPOT

ALFALFA

She would bake us the most delicious muffins! I believe they were raisin bran and carrot muffins—wholesome, lovely, created with care and absolutely fantastic, just like her.

~ Anna Shell

Whether it was a protest or retreat, Michelle gathered the group for centering first. She would ask us what we brought with us and why, and what we left behind (metaphorically too). I still think of that question when setting my intentions.

~ Megan Naseman

Helping others was her passion

Dave Kobersmith

Michelle wasn't afraid to speak up when there was inequality in faculty meetings for staff, but she also expected others to speak up too. There is this look that Michelle would give that almost asked the question, "What are you going to do?"

~Ashley Cochrane

At a mountaintop removal protest, I told Michelle that my friend and I planned to engage in civil disobedience, risking arrest. Michelle's exuberant hug emboldened me to do it.

~ Paige Billman

Her smile carried the weight of the world so you wouldn't have to.

- C. L Eliza Wilde

Acknowlegements

This book would not have been possible without the generous financial support of these donors.

Ashley Cochrane and Jeff From
Betty Hibler
Benjamin McKenzie
Carrie Jadud
Courtney Parrish
Curtis Sandberg
Daneille King
Dave and Kim Kobersmith
Debbi Brock
Deborah Payne
Dorothy Chao
Drew West
Emily LaDouceur
Hazel Morris
Ismaila Ceesay
Jen, Will and Grace Lee
Jeremy S. McQueen

Kate Egerton
Katie Hines
Kent Gilbert
Kris Wilks
Landon Mecham
Lori Myers-Steele
Libby Falk Jones
Martha Thornburgh
Melanie Wilkinson
Neil Mecham
Norina Samuels
Rebecca Nelkie
Sana Khan Jadoon
Sonam Yangzom
Susana Lein

Friends and members
of Union Church

Special Thanks

We would like to acknowledge the long history of feminine community builders and organizers, especially indiginous women and women of color that Michelle Tooley learned from. In her book, "Voices of the Voiceless", Michelle wrote "In Guatemala women have created a community of active participation through involvement in human rights groups. In spite of their lack of power in the public sphere, women are working for justice in a country devastated by violence and poverty. Their actions are self-empowering." Michelle also drew on the work of **Rigoberta Menchu**, winner of the Nobel Peace Prize and author of *I, Rigoberta Menchu: An Indian Woman in Guatemala*.

We would also like to thank the **Kentucky Foundation for Women** for providing an artist enrichment grant to support this work, **Ann Butwell** for allowing the use of her beautiful artwork to be included in this book and for her help along the way, **Ashley Cochrane** for providing material that served as inspiration, **Beth Dotson-Brown** and **Debbi Brock** for their support and guidance, and to the **Sisters of Loretto Motherhouse**, where Michelle was a co-member, for providing source material and a beautiful visit.

Activities to Try

Listening Activity
From Narrative 4, a global organization focused on building empathy around the world.

Michelle listened intently to people she encountered. Listening deeply is a way we build connections to other people. Let's try an experiment with listening! You'll need a partner and a timer. This will take less than 10 minutes. You both need to think about something you really enjoy, something you could talk about for a long time. Got it? Good! Now, choose one person to be the talker and one person to be the listener.

Talker: Talk for 1 minute about the thing you care about! Listener: For 30 seconds, try real hard to listen to what they are saying. Then for the last 30 seconds, pay attention to something else. Then switch! What did you notice? Was it hard to talk when someone wasn't paying attention to you? How did it feel when your partner was listening to you?

Art Activity
Find some things that people might throw away or some things outside- maybe some used paper or toilet paper rolls or some rocks. Use them to create something that shows the world you want to live in. Share what you created with a friend or a family member.

Something to Think About
Michelle showed up for people in a lot of different ways. Sometimes, she just showed up with some cookies. Sometimes she showed up by trying to change rules and laws that hurt people. What are ways that you have seen people show up and help other people? What are ways that you have done this? Make a drawing or create a collage to show the ways the ways you have seen people show up and help others.

Photograph by Samuel Dent

About the Creators

Grace Todd McKenzie is an artist, activist, creator, dreamer, planner, and strategist for justice and joy. She lives in Berea, KY, with her husband, Chris, and their cat, Kindle. She also gives excellent hugs and enjoys sharing good food and conversation.

Heather Dent is a mixed media artist using paper collage and digital art for the illustrations in this book. She is also the founder of Winterberry Studio, where she teaches people how to create their own art using items from nature like pebbles, flower petals, and pinecones.

CPSIA information can be obtained
at www.ICGtesting.com
Printed in the USA
BVHW090200010622
638358BV00002B/29